FOUR SEA~~~
DREA

"A CONCISE
ON POETRY"

Elisa-Nefeli

GW01453063

AN ALBEDO PROJECT PUBLICATION ©

© 2022 ELISA- NEFELI

Unauthorized translation, duplication, photocopying, introduction or distribution partially or fully, under any means, including electronic copying, storage or distribution is a violation of applicable laws. Albedo Project is a trademark and service mark owned by Albedo Project Library all rights reserved. The moral right of Elisa-Nefeli, to be identified as the Author, this work has been asserted in the accordance With the Copyright Designs and Patents Act of 1998All rights reserved. No part of this publication may be reproduced, Stored in a retrieval system, or transmitted in any form or by any means, electronic, mechanical, photocopying, recording, or otherwise, without the prior permission of both the copyright owner and the above publisher of this work. All the characters in this composition are fictitious, and any resemblance to actual persons, living or dead, is purely coincidental.

Table of Content

Acknowledgment

A special acknowledgment to the Amazon Pros team for their help in making this book a reality.

About the Author

Having experienced the hardship of a dictatorship at an early age Elisa-Nefeli decided for a life of action. She advanced in medical studies and the humanities, excelled in different sports and worked in projects relating to arts education self-betterment. She lived across four continents between the West the Far East and Asia. She started writing from an early age. She sees Poetry as painting through words and sharing new vistas.

How the Journey Begun

Welcome to this short journey in the world of poetry.

While there are many works that deal with the various schools of "how to" write poetry, the style, the rhythm, the different forms, this manual goes down to the basics of the basics, way before you get to the various style "dogmas" and schools.

It is concerning that the first stage of getting to know the subject.

Like in music, where you orient yourself to what is a musical instrument or how you can get a sound.

It takes some patience and exercise on the very basics before you can get to the point of playing a tune, and even more like experimenting with different styles.

You may know Pablo Picasso as the founder of a contemporary abstract painting style called "Cubism." But if you take a look further into his work, you will discover that Picasso, from a very early age, has been creating a lot of "classic" sort to say paintings, and once he got that one down well, he then ventured into the creation of the cubism painting style.

If you talk to a violinist or a pianist, you will find that before getting into dealing with tunes and harmonies and songs, they had to drill a lot on their basics, how you place your hands, how you hold the bow, and so on.

The same goes for simple subjects such as driving or cooking. If you do not know the basics and do not possess a basic understanding of how to mix ingredients or how to change gears, your chances of making a good meal or of enjoying a good trip will be rather poor.

I considered that before venturing into the realm of poetic styles, one would need to start from the beginning. So the journey begins by defining the terms and related practical facts that can lead someone to understand and be able to make poetry.

Many times when you try to get to the "how to's" before knowing the "where-to's," you may end up not succeeding or, even worse, end up in a mystery about it. This is when all becomes confusing, and your attempts end up in a trash can with dismay.

In talking with people - and I have had many chances to do that across the planet - I was sometimes amazed as to how, in many a subject, we go on trying to deal with high concepts before putting there some basic data upon which to build on.

In some other universes, all this may be possible, but as far as I observed in the planet we live on and the physical universe we exist, in as most probably spirits "dressed" in the material, I did not see a house being built from the roof down. It always goes from the foundation and then upwards.

When I started to deal with that form of art called poetry from an early age, I started with a simple understanding of my children's experience of poetry.

My first poetic experience could have been said to be the first impressions that reached my forming senses, the sound of the morning, the color of the day, that "wow" my parents expressed to a first smile or to a first touch - as far as I could remember.

Then, as I grew up, there were things that marked me deeply as my own "Wows." The rhythm of life, the harmony between spaces and life forms, and the emotions I could experience.

One of the things that impressed me big time, which I found rather poetic at the time, was this concept I encountered in a children's tale of a magician who could fit everything in a small bag and bring it with him. This was a really big "wow" for me.

I remember calculating how it would be if I could fit an infinity of toys and children's books in a small bag that had no weight. A small bag I could carry everywhere.

Not much later, I discovered my next "wow." I found out that I could express myself through words.

The day I managed that, it was not anymore trying to say something that resulted in a puzzled look from my mother or a father who could not understand what I was talking about. Finally, I discovered a means that made me comprehensible to them and myself. I could say "water" and get "water."

Consequently, I discovered what communication as a word actually meant for me at least: it simply meant "the way of sharing things, to be able to have a common experience or understanding."

Following that discovery, I understood that words were a means to be able to express myself in ways that others could understand, too, which made life much easier. You say "hungry," and you get food. You say "walk," and you are out walking. That marked words and communication for me as a means to a better life and to more freedom.

Years after, it dawned on me that words were invented for that very purpose - to share experiences and understanding.

If you multiply that fact by the number of people who want to express themselves and all ethnicities and cultures around the world, you end up on a planet like ours where there are 180 main languages available for use and over 9000 dialects. But aside from the great numbers of diversity. The purpose of words and language remains the same even when they are so many different languages.

The means differ from area to area, but that does not change the use.

That awareness made me fond of words. I did not care if I would make orthographic errors or if my grammar would not be perfect.

The first thing that I saw mattered was to be able to communicate at the start somehow or anyhow and then raise the standard from there.

What mattered was to say it and say it and say it until I said it better. I am not saying this is the way to go about it. All I am saying is that it was a practical way to go about it.

And so it was at the age of six that I wrote my first poem. I recall that we were given homework as kindergartners. Some of my friends protested heavily on the task, but for me, that was the best homework I could have experienced a real word challenge.

The subject was "my family." I had fun taking a big subject such as family and trying to express it in a few words, all harmonized together and delivered with rhythm and spark.

That day among pen and paper, I thought I had found my own magic bag where no matter the size of the idea, it could all fit nicely in the space of a few words. I remember running in and out of my room, reading the words to my mom to see if she was getting it, and by the time I went to sleep, the poem was all written and ready to go.

I could not wait to bring my very first poem to my teacher. I recall being so excited. I carefully took my notebook containing this precious piece of what I considered a masterpiece in the making, and I offered it with a big smile to my kindergartner teacher.

In my little head, I was sure that all this work would have bought me a lot of admiration and congrats that day – something really worth living for.

To my surprise, my expectations were far off. That little poem gave me a reprimand from an angry teacher who, after reading it, turned toward me, telling me in a loud voice for all to hear how I did not write it. It was impossible that at this age, I could write something so sophisticated that my mother wrote it for me and that I was - an unethical little scam, in other words.

Alas. My dream of glory became my worst nightmare. My poetic and communication wings shrunk. That feeling of being as big as life (that the ability to express yourself can give) got squashed down to a space comparable to that of a tiny ant.

I took my notebook with my head down as I let some tears run down my cheek, but without saying more, I picked up myself from the "ashes" and went back home.

That day I got my firsthand experience of the words "criticism," "illogic," and "invalidation."

That live demonstration of "animated words" made me realize that when you deal with communication, you are dealing as well with the ideas and limitations of the reality of an audience that can be as warm as winter in Alaska.

Thanks to my somehow resilient nature and thanks to the compassion and support of my family and friends, I managed to overcome this first poetic delusion.

That made me consider not publishing my poetic work in the world of grown-ups prior to becoming a grown-up myself – just to fit the "ethnic" requirements and tolerance of the audience.

It contributed as well to my deciding then that part of being a poet contains an important part. Knowing what your reader's reality is and how to be able to communicate with that reality too. As communication is more fun when it is not from you to you after all.

It was for me time to get to know the subject better for myself if I wanted to live happily thereafter with this passion of mine.

Funny enough, I kept that first poem which I still have somewhere with the children's letter look and its old fading paper, as a reminder of how surprising life can sometimes be, and I went on discovering for myself what poetry is all about.

The discovery went step by step and was completed by the time I finished writing "Four Seasons of Dreams," which is why this "Concise Manual" remained an integral part of the work.

I am sharing my discoveries with you now. They are not absolute or official discoveries. They are simple, practical discoveries that can help you the way they helped me.

I wish you a lot of fun going through them and working with them.

Despite the difficulties, the good thing about poetry is that you can always write a poem, even about your unhappy moments or a nasty rebuff, and get over it all. It is an expression of one's understanding, and expression has a healing factor for one.

What is Poetry After All?

How can I increase my own skills on it?

To be able to understand poetry and its use, one has to look at its source and origin. In short, one could say when "you speak or deal with something," it may be better that you know what you are talking about.

The word itself Poetry is derived from the Greek word "Poeio," which means create. So Poetry means simply "a creation".

That means that if you look at the origin of the word, the way a person dresses can be poetry, the way one walks can be poetry, the way one lives life can be poetry, and the way one arranges one's furniture can be poetry.

The moment something is created, it is, by definition, a work of poetry. This is the origin of the word.

Today in the more common sense, the word poetry is said to refer to "a (written) work of poetry – the art of rhythmical composition".

This could be said to be the transcribed experience on paper through words of creation.

So here you deal with the worded aspect of experiencing a creation or perceiving mentally or through one's senses.

In other words, by clearing the meaning and origin of the word, I realized that while painting could be said to put in two dimensions, a creation of color and form, and music, the harmonic combination of sound, and photography a way of writing in two dimensions through light, poetry is painting with words. This includes the harmonic combination of words, the rhythm of words, etc.

So how does that knowledge help one with poetry?

First, it gives you the field of experience. You can increase your sense of creation by paying attention to things created and looking at the effects things have on the relations and differences.

The way a photographer may increase his skill of photography by observing spaces and colors and relations and character and thus gaining the ability to create a photo that will have an impact. A poet could increase their ability to express things by increasing his experience of perceiving and observing the living.

The way you need to learn the different letters of the alphabet and their possible combinations, you learn the different types of creations life offers you.

This includes the observation of rhythm. Life and living have rhythm music has a rhythm and poetry too. There can be a fast pace, a slow pace, and a dying pace. Whichever pace you want to use. There is a cadence and a rhythm in poetry.

And once you have done that and you can now discern creations, relations, rhythm, symphonies, and cacophonies comes the next stage of learning your "notes." These are the words.

If you want to deal with words and compose poetry, you need to learn words. You need to learn to work with words the way a painter gets to practice his colors, the musician gets to practice his notes the photographer gets to know the laws of light and images.

That does not mean you need to know thousands and thousands of words before using these to express yourself. You can start writing poetry by knowing a few words, as long as you know what you are expressing and the reader can understand what you are talking about.

What I did that worked for me was to make each word my word. I did that by using a word in sentences, by making sketches of words, by writing words in different styles till I knew I had the hang of it like a basketball player learns and then controls his basketball.

So once you got that far here comes the next ingredient. Paper and pen. You get a good amount of paper and some pens, and you can start your journey.

You can then make games with words like I used to do. You choose 5 or 10 words, and with your friends, you play using these words in different sentences till you are able to use them with ease.

Or you can play who gets the best word to express an idea or concept.

Learn how to say things by their name. Take a visual dictionary -if you do not have one, the library may have- and learn how things are called so you can describe them.

Start the drill by describing your room, your desk, your bed, or your cat.

The more you do that, the easier words will come the way a musician gets more and more skilled with his notes.

This is the first basic skill. You can learn all the technical details of how to write, but first, you need to know how to use your notes, in that case – words.

Then start playing with them. You can express gloomy thoughts, light thoughts, or amusing words. You start learning the different tones of thoughts you want to express.

You can do it as a game for fun. You can get with friends and name a subject and start writing something suspenseful about it or something scary or something sad or something happy.

And once you have gotten that far, do not forget to drill your ability to change perspective. As you deal with creation, increasing the skill of viewing things from different perspectives will help you in your freedom of expression.

This is the first basic that I saw working, and it works for words the way it works for any human skill, such as walking, talking, running, biking, climbing, and driving. You start to get some basic skills, and then you get it to the next level.

What can poetry help me with?

I discovered that poetry could help you with a lot of things. It can have a healing effect on you. As water can run and clean dirt, so can expression lessen the harm or pain, or distress.

It can have a soothing effect when you need something to appease your distress or stress.

It can help you understand something better

It can help you elate something.

There are many uses. And there is no fixed standard in the art of what is good or bad. Like truth is a relative value.

If someone reads a poem and from apathy feels grief rather well, this is a bit better an emotion probably – it is still a step up, a bettering in a way.

This planet, although small and rather pretty, takes some confronting. There are good things and ugly things. One can express different realities and states of things.

The only point I want to make on this is that as the nature of poetry is the creation and as it is what it means, the key point is to keep it on the level of creation and not use it for destruction. It is not the purpose of this form of art.

What it expresses can be different. Through practical experience, I noticed that when you work with poetry, you often use observation and imagination. The imagination of how to combine things and create things.

One then uses rhythm, harmony, and impact to put these words together.

The fact of observing and using your imagination more often can help you in life. It can help you see things better. If you do not observe a pole as you walk, you may bump onto it, so the ability to observe is an important ability for every aspect of life.

Sometimes I consider people look too much into their thoughts for answers instead of looking at what is really there to solve in the real world.

The increase of the ability to imagine things or a combination of things helps you gain the ability to solve better things in life.

So aside from increasing your skills with poetry, you can increase skills in life through it.

You can learn to experience the moments of life when you learn to perceive them, and you learn to validate them. Very often, I find in the rhythm and struggles of life, we forget to experience the moments. However, these moments are life and living, so one has to learn to go for achievement without forgetting to value the moments, and poetry can help you do that.

One can create a message that can have an impact that can better a culture.

In my early years in difficult moments, there have been the words of skilled poets that helped me live through them and keep in mind that the way a diamond looks ugly when surrounded by carbon and earth, one has to find the value which lies beyond the apparent dirt.

Through the ages, you can see how poetry has had the power to change and enhance our culture. This is because even the thickest granite or steel that can stop an object cannot stop, and ideas, when absorbed by others, can become a future reality.

One of the earliest religious and philosophical poems, the Tao Te King of Lao Tse ("The Way of The Nature and the Wise"), expressed concepts about the truths of wisdom and nature in 81 verses. These 81 verses have affected generations upon generations of humans.

Moreover, in the Asian culture, this endeavor of bettering oneself in the art of words was considered to bring more understanding or to appease violence.

In fact, in the code of the Samurai, it was considered that a Samurai, in times of peace, should indulge in poetry and writing to elevate its spirits and to increase sensitivity to the values of life.

In other circumstances, like in the Zen philosophies, short verses were considered to help to bring about a better spiritual condition.

In the middle ages, the Italian poet Dante Alighieri used poetry to raise awareness of the political and social conditions of his contemporary life.

There are many such examples in history.

Today the most common popular acclaim of poetry could be the song lyrics. They may not always be the best, but they do spread concepts for the better or, the worse. In fact, the combination of two arts, the one of poetry and the one of sound and music, has proven rather powerful.

There are different techniques. William Shakespeare wrote in a very precise verse type, and like in music and in painting, there are all kinds of the opinion of what is good or bad.

The key point is to see that concepts communicated through poetry can become a means of cultural awareness but can also entertain or soothe.

While the clocks upon this planet keep ticking, while we follow the set rhythm of everyday living, while vested interests may toss us sometimes around, like leaves in the winds of the unknown, there is something which will always be there within us as an inherent potential of creating. Our own ability to express ourselves. Our own poetic skills.

Poetry, like any aesthetic art, remembers and operates at the level of creation. And this is the highest state one can reach.

How do you know if your poetry is good? What is good for you is good for you to begin with. And once you are satisfied with your own work, then tell it to the man on the street. Can he appreciate it? If not, go back to the beginning.

While writing poetry may help you, do not forget that it is communication; it is read by someone, and it has to impact that person.

Once I Have Got My Basics Established

Where do I go from there?

Once you learn to deal with your basics, you will need to start working with the message. What is the message you want to express, and is it what you wrote communicating that message?

If you wrote it for yourself to discharge. This is good for you, but if you want to have a bigger impact, you need to learn to address an audience. Decide what type of people are your audience and how you could communicate with them.

Then you need to move toward more professional standards. Learn the different types of poetry. The Haiku, the classic one, the surrealistic one.

See which one fits you best and get to know how to increase your skill.

Here enters grammar. It helps you to relate words together so that they can be better understood.

Reading other poets enriches your experience.

And more than anything, remember that while poetry deals in the field of aesthetics, it is keeping a culture alive, keeping the language alive, and can create dreams and visions of what will be our tomorrow.

So keep at it, work at it, and even if a teacher or loved one may tell you they do not believe you created the poem or someone did not like it. The important is to create and enjoy creating.

These are the very basics I wanted to share with you:

What poetry really means.

How to increase awareness of words and environments through observation, perspective, rhythm, and relation of words and words themselves.

Some of the uses of poetry and the role of a poet in keeping a culture alive and feeding it with dreams and visions may enhance human existence and relations.

And do not forget that skill and ability increase by practice so write and write and write till you get to the point that a concert pianist may get.

It is a skill, it is an ability, and the more you practice, the better you can become.

I wanted to share these few points with you concerning some basics of poetry, which I wish they will assist you in your own poetry journey.

Here below, you will find a space where you can begin your own poetry practice. Over to you for a great journey.

Elisa- Nefeli

CPSIA information can be obtained
at www.ICGtesting.com
Printed in the USA
BVHW060036091122
651449BV00011B/482

9 781915 662712